Breath of Song

10 works by women composers for unaccompanied SATB choir

Compiled and edited by
SARAH QUARTEL

MUSIC DEPARTMENT

OXFORD
UNIVERSITY PRESS

OXFORD
UNIVERSITY PRESS

Great Clarendon Street, Oxford OX2 6DP,
United Kingdom

Oxford University Press is a department of the University of Oxford.
It furthers the University's objective of excellence in research, scholarship,
and education by publishing worldwide. Oxford is a registered trade mark of
Oxford University Press in the UK and in certain other countries

Database right Oxford University Press (maker)

First published 2021

Impression: 1

ISBN 978-0-19-353202-1

Music and text origination by Julia Bovee
Printed in Great Britain on acid-free paper by
Halstan & Co. Ltd, Amersham, Bucks.

Preface

In response to a growing demand for pieces by women composers, I was invited by Oxford University Press to assemble a collection of outstanding new works from living contributors. This set me on an exciting journey of discovery as I sought out new composers from across the world and had the opportunity to connect with others I've long admired.

Breath of Song brings together ten compelling works from different creators, some of whom are well-known, and others are just beginning to make their mark on the international choral scene. Each piece contributed to shaping this collection and played a part in refining the parameters of the original brief. In *Breath of Song* we have a group of unaccompanied works appropriate for concert performance and at a difficulty level accessible to the majority of choirs. Sacred and secular texts are both represented, and pieces can be programmed individually or together in one thrilling concert. Each work has a unique story to tell and brings something fresh and exciting to the contemporary choral catalogue. From the modal sound coloured by the Hindustani classical tradition in Esmail's 'TāReKiṬa', to the expressive melodic lines seasoned with Scottish snaps in McDowall's 'God be with us', there is something in this eclectic collection for each choir, each concert, and each season.

Thank you to Robyn Elton, Commissioning Editor at Oxford University Press, for her tireless work on this project and for amplifying voices that deserve to be heard. Thank you to Amy Chang and Jane Griffiths for keen eyes and thoughtful editing. Finally, thank you to my fellow composers for sharing your music and for trusting us with your exquisite work.

Sarah Quartel
November 2020

Contents

Notes on the pieces

Wake, Love, Wake!   *Joan Szymko*

This is an emotive and rich setting of an exquisite text by Rabindranath Tagore. There is tremendous opportunity for word-painting right from the beginning. Feeling and expressing the emotion behind each word will make for an impactful singing experience and moving performance. Though much of the piece is marked *pp*, *p*, and *mp*, there is room for great range within these dynamics. Use consonants to project and help keep the sound lifted in quieter moments. Relaxing into the end of descending phrases will allow the music to land with the text and the piece's impactful message to be felt.

My beloved spake   *Becky McGlade*

McGlade's setting of this well-known passage from Song of Songs is warm and evocative. Moments of tenderness and intimacy in the text are brought to the fore as singers maintain connectivity by breathing together at the same speed, and moving as one through moments of subtle tempo change. Take care with triplets throughout, ensuring that enough time is given and they are not rushed. Excellent in a concert setting, this piece is suitable for a larger group as well as an unconducted small ensemble.

God be with us   *Cecilia McDowall*

'God be with us' has a graceful and meditative quality. Expressive and flowing melodic lines float between voices creating a gentle sense of push and pull. Use the breath throughout to keep the sound buoyant and to support the stillness and sustain found in the writing. Notice the contrast between the legato lines and the clear rhythm of the Scotch snaps. Always accent the snaps, as is noted in the score. There are many moments to enjoy—relax into dissonances and lean into suspensions. This piece would be suitable in both liturgical and concert settings.

TāReKiṮa   *Reena Esmail*

This is an exciting piece that feels tremendously satisfying to sing when performance is rooted in knowing it deeply. It is in a rāga (a melodic framework similar to a mode) called Jog, which incorporates both major and minor modalities into a single scale. The text syllables are onomatopoeic vocalizations of the sounds produced by Hindustani (north Indian classical) instruments. At first glance the text may look daunting to those unfamiliar with these vocalizations but, at closer look, you will see that there are only three different patterns of text throughout the piece. These patterns are easy to master when learned by ear and repeated aloud. Instructions detailing how to access the composer's video pronunciation guide can be found in the score. This piece would make a bright and energizing close to any concert.

Love Letter   *Sarah Dacey*

'Love Letter' is set in a gently rocking 5/8 metre and features captivating harmonic language that is intriguing yet accessible. The light divisi in soprano and alto parts is well within the reach of community choirs. Watch that the opening 'mm' is not a percussive 'hmm' but rather embodies a warm and supportive foundation. Close attention to dynamics throughout, particularly on the first page, will help capture the ebb and flow in the writing by placing weight and understanding on significant words in the text.

The Arrow and the Song   *Laura Hawley*

With a strong melody and a grooving rhythmic accompaniment, 'The Arrow and the Song' is a distinctive setting of Longfellow's text that is very satisfying to sing. Equally enjoyable in the hands of a small ensemble or full choir, this piece is set in a contemporary *a cappella* style with some pop inflections. In passages with ostinati, be careful to maintain pitch integrity by keeping lift and spin in the voice. It may be helpful for singers to notice how their riff is reframed when the harmony underneath changes while their ostinato remains the same.

The Birds' Lullaby   *Sarah Quartel*

This is a playful yet tender piece with a singable melody and dancing scat accompaniment. It would work well for either full choir or a small ensemble. In the chorus section, go right to the 'ng' sound on 'sing' and 'swing' to keep the music rhythmic and light. Take care to remain casual on the 'd' of 'doo' and do not enunciate crisply. It should feel free and easy. This piece would work well on any programme celebrating nature, spring, or Earth Day.

Snow is Silent   *Jenny Mahler*

This dynamic and engaging piece is filled with character. The excitement of the work is deepened through the use of body percussion, quick contrasting dynamics, and passages with vocal sound effects. Experiment with the placement of singers in the performance space to further enjoy the dramatic possibilities of the piece. Pay attention to how the composer has set vibrant words in the text such as 'kerfuffle', 'commotion', and 'splash'. Be sure to follow all articulations, dynamics, and written instructions in order to capture the full effect. This work would be excellent as a conclusion to a first half or as a concert closer.

O ye who taste that Love is sweet   *Eleanor Daley*

This hymn-like setting of Christina Rossetti's secular text about love would be meaningful at a wedding or within a concert programmed around a variety of themes, including Christmas. While not difficult, the work is expertly crafted with each voice receiving an engaging part. Creative staging such as singing in the round or from a balcony would be comfortable and attainable with this piece. Maintain the air-flow through rising sections of eighth notes and move here with breath-filled propulsion, rather than acceleration.

Round me falls the night   *Annabel Rooney*

The atmosphere is instantly set in the opening bars of this shining piece. One can immediately envision a beautiful evening emerging as the brightness of day softens into dusk. Rooney makes excellent use of the full range of all voice types, capitalizing on colours available in higher versus lower registers. Be sure to keep the vowel light in words such as 'done' and 'none' which sit lower in the range. Enjoy the harmonic shifts throughout and bring out moments in which one voice moves in a contrasting rhythm from the others. This piece would be lovely in both church and concert settings.

Sarah Quartel

All of the pieces in this anthology are also available separately from the OUP website and participating digital retailers.

Wake, Love, Wake!

Rabindranath Tagore
(1861–1941)

JOAN SZYMKO
(b. 1957)

Duration: 3 mins

brim my emp-ty cup, fill my emp-ty cup,

brim my emp-ty cup, fill my emp-ty cup, and

brim my emp-ty cup, fill my cup,

brim my emp-ty cup, fill my cup,

and with a breath of song ruf-fle the night.

with a breath of song_____ ruf-fle the night.

a breath of song_____ ruf-fle the night.

of song ruf-fle the night.

My beloved spake

Song of Songs 2: 10–12

BECKY McGLADE
(b. 1974)

Duration: 3.5 mins

for Val Withams

God be with us

Invocation, *Carmina Gadelica*, Vol. 1
Alexander Carmichael
(1832–1912)

CECILIA McDOWALL
(b. 1951)

For a video pronunciation guide led by Reena Esmail, please visit www.oup.co.uk/tarekita

PRONUNCIATION GUIDE

Vowels
ā as in c**a**r
a as in **a**bout
e as in f**e**d
i as in s**i**t
ī as in tr**ee**
ō as in n**o**te
ŭ as in g**oo**d
u as in th**u**mb
ū as in f**oo**d

Consonants (when different from English pronunciation)
t as in **the** (dental) *
d as in the Spanish word **d**os or **d**ón**d**e (dental)
r as in the Spanish word **r**ojo or **r**osa (flipped)

Sounds with no equivalents in Romance languages
To make the sound "Dh":
• touch your tongue to your teeth, as if you were saying the word "the" (dental consonant)
• as you say the consonant, push extra air through it (if you hold your palm a few inches in front of your mouth, you should be able to feel a puff of air)

To make the sound "ṭ":
• curl your tongue back, so the underside of the tip is touching the top of your mouth (retroflex consonant)
• then bring it forward to pronounce the ṭ

* The "t" is the most critical consonant to pronounce correctly in this piece. If one singer in the choir uses a conventional English "t" sound, it will drown out the subdued attack of all the other dental "t"s.

for Urban Voices Project

TāReKiṬa
(तारेकिट)

Words and music by
REENA ESMAIL
(b. 1983)

* close to m immediately

Duration: 2 mins

* Grace notes should only be sung by a few singers per section.

* Low basses may sing an octave lower for the remainder of the piece, if desired.

for Richard and Teresa

Love Letter

Edna St Vincent Millay
(1892–1950)

SARAH DACEY
(b. 1979)

Duration: 3 mins

* Keyboard reduction for rehearsal only.

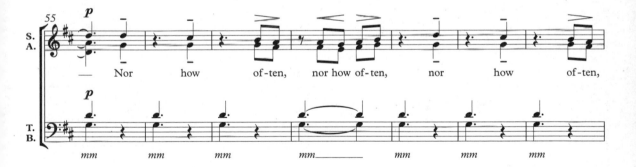

you and me, with you and me, you and me, you and

do with you and me, and me, you and me, you and

me, with you and me, and me, you and me, you and

you, with you and me, and me, you and me, you and

me, and me, you and me, you and you and

me, and me, and me, and you me, and me.

me, you and me.

me.

Commissioned in 2016 by the Savridi Singers of Calgary and their artistic director, Erica Phare-Bergh,
for the occasion of the choir's 30th anniversary

The Arrow and the Song

Henry Wadsworth Longfellow
(1807–82)

LAURA HAWLEY
(b. 1982)

Before the notes begin, start with *c.*15–20 seconds of some voices imitating the sounds of wind, gentle breezes, the subtle whistle of an arrow, and occasional bird calls. Continue the wind and birds (or wind only) until the text begins in b. 13. Choirs should feel free to experiment with placement of singers, textural variety, and character and 'pitch' of the wind and bird sounds according to their own artistic expressive nuance.

* straight to the '*n*' of '*doon*'

† The piano reduction includes the rhythmic accompanying parts throughout; for reason of playability, melodic lines are sometimes omitted.

Also available separately in a version for SSSAAA unaccompanied (ISBN 978–0–19–355088–9). Duration: 4 mins

* 'du' should sound like 'doo'

* straight to the 'm' of doom

* A few voices from each section leave the pitch and make the unvoiced wind sound: '*haaaaAAAaaaaah*'

The Birds' Lullaby

E. Pauline Johnson
(1861–1913)

SARAH QUARTEL
(b. 1982)

This piece is also available in a version for SSAA unaccompanied (ISBN 978–0–19–352466–8).

Duration: 3 mins

Snow is Silent

John Pickles
(b. 1953)

JENNY MAHLER
(b. 1989)

Duration: 2.5 mins

*   = rub palms together

**   = click fingers

† = stamp feet (left, right)

* straight to 'sh' of 'splash'

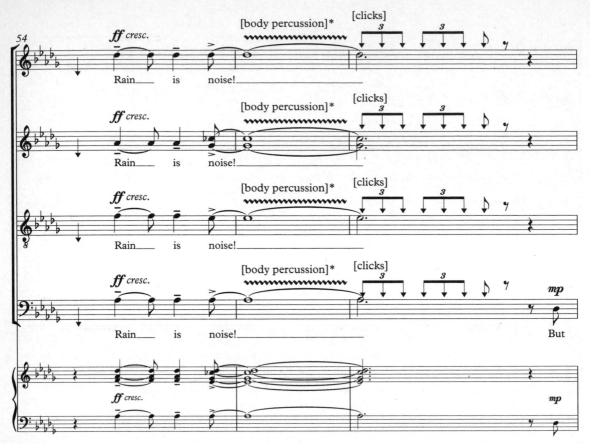

*   〰〰〰〰 = cacophony of clicks and thigh-slaps in free rhythm

Written for the wedding of Laura Pedersen and Christopher Bowman, 8 July 2006

O ye who taste that Love is sweet

Christina Rossetti
(1830–94)

ELEANOR DALEY
(b. 1955)

* Keyboard reduction for rehearsal only.

Duration: 3 mins

up___ and won-der,___ and draw   near.   _oo_____

up___ and won-der,___ and draw_ near.   _oo_____

and draw   near.   _oo_____

_oo_____

O   ye   who taste   that   Love___   is   sweet.

O   ye   who   taste   that   Love___   is_   sweet.

O   ye   who   taste_ that_   Love___   is___   sweet.

O   ye who   taste   that   Love   is   sweet.

Round me falls the night

William Romanis
(1824–99)

ANNABEL McLAUCHLAN ROONEY
(b. 1973)

Duration: 3 mins

Round me falls the night has been recorded by The Choir of Christ's College, Cambridge, conducted by David Rowland, on the album *As a seed bursts forth* (Regent).